DRIFTWOOD

Prayers for Beached Travelers

DON KIMBALL

PAULIST PRESS
New York/Mahwah, NJ

Library of Congress Cataloging-in-Publication Data

Kimball, Don, 1943–
    Driftwood : prayers for beached travelers / Don Kimball.
        p.   cm.
    ISBN 0-8091-3578-7 (alk. paper)
    1. Prayers.   I. Title.
  BV245.K543   1995
  242'.8—dc20   95-2882
                                                   CIP

Published by Paulist Press
997 Macarthur Boulevard
Mahwah, New Jersey 07430

Printed and bound in the
United States of America

Table of Contents

PART ONE—p. 1

PART TWO—p. 49

PART THREE—p. 97

PART FOUR—p. 147

SPECIAL THANKS TO:

Tom Farrell, for giving this book a life;
Marlita Rowan, for giving it a future;
Maryanne Hoburg, for giving it maturity;
Lawrence Boadt, C.S.P., for bringing it into the Now Age.

PART ONE:

EXPECTATIONS, FRUSTRATIONS, MOOD TIDES, QUESTIONS

Expectations

Expectations

Funny thing about my life:
  funny thing about the way I deal with people:

I just can't help walking into a relationship
  without laying a heap of expectations
  on the other person.

Expectations are patches of dissatisfaction
  on my quilt of anticipation.

They amount to conditional acceptance . . .
  love with a hidden agenda:

    You must meet my expectations.
    You must meet my needs,
      Or
    I won't play with you.

    Of course,
    I may never even tell you
      what my expectations are,
        But you'd better come through.

If by chance you stumble into meeting
  my "requirements" for a relationship,
    then I feel good.

The only trouble is that
  I love the feelings I'm having around you
  more than I really love you.

I'm still far away from meeting the real you.

And you are even farther away from meeting the real me.

Expectations are such corrosive things.

If they don't destroy a relationship before it starts,
    they see to it that they keep me far
        from a true encounter
            with the other person.

Lord, maybe that's why I've
    never,
    ever,
    really met
    you.

Still Unsatisfied

Rivers filled with flashing fish.

Clouds filled with electric vapors.

Trees filled with teeming populations.

Rocks filled with terrestrial vibrations.

   What are we filled with?

Vineyards and fields filled with yellow mustard,
   as if someone had broken eggs
      all over the landscape.

A neglected rail fence staggers down the hill,
   its gaps unable any longer
      to accomplish
         its mission
         of partition.

What makes us grasp out,
   unsatisfied,
      for more love,
      for more life,
      for more meaning?

Already, it's going to be a hair-flying,
   coat-tossing day
      as the pre-dawn wind
         waltzes the rain across the road.

Just as the Unsatisfied Darkness
        searches for Light
            to unlock its contents,
        the Unsatisfied Person
            seeks love,
                life in its fullness.

We won't settle for anything else.

    Why should we?

Traveling

Lord, I'm on a big trip.

I'm a busy person.

I've got places to go,
  people to see,
  things to do.

I haven't got time to listen.

  Just time to tell you that
    I've got a great plan for this world,
    a plan that can't miss
    if I could just get around to the right people.

It's all in whom you know,
  not what you know.

And Lord,
  since you and I are pretty good friends,
    I was wondering if
    you wouldn't mind
    using your influence
      to rearrange the world
      to suit my plans.

My plan calls for
  getting myself around to enough people
  and telling them
    to stop hurting one another,
    that life can have meaning
      if they will only listen to me.

I could be the key to their happiness,
 and the center of their lives.

To be honest, Lord,
 the plan hasn't worked very well so far.

  People don't seem to like my plan.
  They'd like to get rid of me,
   so I need a little help from you.

What?

What did you say?

What do you mean
 there's only room for one Messiah around here?

Now

For some people,
   there's always a Tomorrow,
   never a Today.
      Day-care children preparing for school,
         next year;
      first-graders preparing for adolescence,
         only a couple of years away.
      teenagers preparing for adulthood,
         artificially induced;
      adults preparing for a new prosperity
         that may never come.

But who is prepared for the Now?

Who is prepared for now days and nights,
      for now flowers,
      for now sunsets,
      for now people,
      and now discoveries?

Lord,
   sometimes I spend all my energies
      coping for tomorrow's possibilities,
   and miss today's opportunities
      that were yesterday's possibilities.

When am I going to learn
   that the best preparation for tomorrow
      is a full life today?

When will I stop praying
   for you to do something
      that's really mine to do?

How can I prepare
      for your coming tomorrow
   if I ignore
      your arrival today?

Let me hear your voice.

   NOW.

MESSAGE

The next time

    I look

        for God,

            I won't think.

                I'll listen.

Frustrations

Battered Around

I saw a Ping-Pong match today, Lord,
    and I think I know how that ball feels:
        tossed back and forth,
        at the mercy of someone else's game.

I saw my life tossed around:
    disregarded by some,
    played with by others,
    given recognition only when
        someone else
            wants to play games.

Lord,
    I don't want to be used;
    I want to be loved.

It occurred to me that
    we should use things and love people,
        not use people and love things.

I hate games people play,
    everybody's games,
    and especially my own games,
        whether it's using people as things,
            or running in circles,
            or spacing out in escapes,
            or hiding behind masks.

Lord, will you be real enough to me
    so I can be real to myself
        and to others?

No games, Lord.

Just love me as I am
   so I can do it too.

I'm having a bad day.

And I don't want to be played with anymore.

Boomerang

Lord, I'd like to see a few changes around here.

I'd like to have the world live
  in an atmosphere of change
    where things I don't like
      would give way
        to new, better ways of doing things.

I'd like to take all the polluting industries
  and put them out of business,
    so I could breathe again.

I'd make teachers more responsive to my needs,
  so I could learn again.

I'd make politicians quit playing with my mind,
  so I could understand again.

I'd take hypocrisy out of the churches,
  and drunks out of cars,
  and exploitation out of the ghettos.

I'd make a lot of changes
  if you'd give me some of that power
    you never seem
      to use.

Why, then, Lord, do you turn on me
  in the face of all this chaos
    and ask *me* to change?

Look at the mess out there!!

Why do I have to do all the changing?

I'd rather rid the world of other people's pollution
   instead of mine.

Here I want to fix up this world right.

And YOU want ME
   to respond to other people's needs,
   to quit playing with their minds,
   to deal with my own hypocrisy,
      drinking,
         and
      exploitation.

Why do you make changing so hard???

Off the Hook

My attitude,
  like the weather,
  is blah,
  with intermittent yuk.

I'm sitting on this dead telephone.

Only moments ago,
  the line was open,
    we were in touch;
      you and I shared what was real.
And now,
  for no reason,
    you're gone,
      like the winter sun
      falling asleep before dinner.

It was my need to journey inward
  that brought me to open the conversation,
  dialing the code that spoke your name.

Was it something I said?

Was it something I did?

Why did you hang up?

    It was just getting good.
    And there was more to say.

This really bothers me.

I'm confused.

My soul is dark.

Please, Lord,

Answer the phone.

What Do They Want?

I know sometimes my head isn't on straight,
    and
I know that my friends are the ones
    who know it first.
        I can tell by the way they "circle" around me,
            waiting for their chance to dart in.

It's really hard inside to look out from my creepy eyes
    upon people around me
    and figure them out.
        What is my relationship with them?
        What do they want from me?

It's even harder with a God whom I can't really see.

What does this God want?

What am I doing here anyway?

Why should I have to do anything for others?

If God is almighty, then I'm not really needed.

And where do I put this strange invitation of Jesus?

  A man who says he came down from heaven,
    so that I could be a partner with him.
      Partner?
      In what?
        Something about "loving one another."
        Something about spreading around what he brought.

I spread something around sometimes,
but it's usually not what he brought.

I wonder if Jesus really does need me or need anybody?

If he does, I'd better start trying a little harder.
I don't think right now I make a very good partner.

Maybe
if I could just get in touch with what he's put inside me,
Maybe
that would do it.

But I'm always
the last one to know
when I do it
right.

Relationships

What is it about a relationship
  that makes it
    so important in the
      discovery of God?

Is it because
  relationships raise feelings?

And in discovering my feelings,
  I discover my needs?

And my needs point
  to where I have to grow?

And growth
  points
    to
      God . . .

Mood Tides

Ocean Message

The ocean is an emperor of many moods:
  one day peaceful,
    mellow,
      its surf a rainbow of soapy bubbles
        dancing across the dishwater;
  another day wild,
    aggressive,
    accusatory,
      like a back seat driver
      with a sore throat.

Frankly, I'm fascinated.

  I want to come to understand this complex, oversized pond
  of thundering waves and gentle mist.

  I know somehow that at the core of its
    capricious fits
  and playful swells
    lies a treasure chest of secrets
      that can introduce me
      to myself
      and
      the meaning of life.

An ocean cannot be owned or harnessed;
  its roaring temper must never be scolded.

When relating to an ocean,
  I must learn how to wait,
    listen,

ponder,
and marvel
at the busy regeneration going on before me
and
within me.

This is a sea that has fed me,
carried me,
terrified me,
and
entertained me.

But I come back today for only one reason:
my ocean has called me to freedom,
to relationship
to Life.

Changing Cycles

Some days, there's not a sky in the clouds.

Other days, the sky is blue and vast
   like a multi-dimensional sea,
      the clouds processing like white icebergs:
         glistening sails
         with no hulls
           and
         no wakes.

Change is everywhere
   like
   the
   colors.

Life is shaded,
   traded,
   complicated.

The stages of our lives
   move
      like the seasons:
         gently at times,
         violent here and there;

         but always determined
           to speak
           one
           clear
           message:
           Life leads to Death.

Death leads to New Life.
Death is not the end of Life.
New Life is the end of Death.

To enter the cycle,
  one must know
    when to go up the mountain
      and
    when to come down.

Stuck in the Middle

Walls have always had ears.

But lately, my ears have walls.

What do I do
    when a relationship seems to go
      up and down,
      back and forth?

I wish I could lose my temper,
      and never find it again.

What do I do
    when the other person's feelings
      aren't the same
        from day to day?

    How do I make contact?

It seems to get more complicated when my own feelings
    aren't the same
      from day to day.

One day I close my eyes,
    and the other person is there,
      but there's still a lot of pain
        rattling in my back porch consciousness,
        like rain
          dripping cowbell tears
          down a rusty drainpipe.

How do I do my confrontations in life?
   With my eyes open?
   or
   With them shut?

And what do I do
   when I'm really not sure
      if I love this person
         anymore?

Summer

It's summer, Lord,

   and that lazy feeling is coming back.

Summer is the time for
  aimless walks
    through rambling fields,

  taking time to watch
    jackrabbits and bees,

  whole acres of curiosity.

I'm curious about their careless existence.

All they seem to need is food.

And they're wondering
  what I'm doing here.

You said something about the lilies of the field once,
  how they don't work
  and are still cared for,
  yeah,
  and about sparrows,
    and how I'm worth
      more than hundreds of them.

Did you really mean that?

You mean, I don't have to earn your love?

Just take it?
    Free?
    That's all right!

It's summer, Lord.

And I don't feel like working anyway.

I could use a little of that unearned love right now.

Maybe that's what I've been missing in my life.

Questions

Are You Still Upset?

Are you still upset?

Then walk the beach with me
  under the washed denim sky.

Talk to me about your hurt.

I will listen to your story,
  understand your words
    and dream with you of some ways
      to retire your anger with a pension.

And as we walk,
  notice that the sea is still running;
    they haven't turned it off.

Behold the waves body-surfing their way to shore,

  the gulls hang-gliding on invisible currents of air,

  the clamshells yawning on the beach,

  the craggy rocks still pounded rhythmically by the sea,
    with pock-marked jaws set to meet life like a plow,
      though molded smooth around the edges
      and
      sculpted by the calculated assaults
      and moody fits of the waves.

There is enough energy on this beach
　　to power-wash
　　　　or
　　occasionally blast
　　　　the whole world from its cares.

Walk back with me, now,
　　along this beach as evening approaches.

We will reprint our footsteps erased hours ago by the rising tide.

And as the sun on the horizon abandons us,
　　remember:
　　I am your friend.

You may tell me anything,
　　and I will understand.

Help

When it comes to needing others,
   I'm not too dependent.

   I like to be on top of things:
      in football, I'm the quarterback;
      in groups, I'm the leader;
      at dances, I'm the D.J.;
      on the highway, I'm in the fast lane;
      in relationships, I'm . . .
         well,
         I'm not so sure.

   I guess I want to be in charge
      stay in control,
         so I won't be hurt,
            surprised,
            mishandled.

   If I put myself in someone else's hands,
      I might be dropped.

   I don't want to bounce on the concrete,
      so I don't surrender my feelings
         to anyone.

   I don't admit I ever need anything,
      so I don't have to ask for help.

So, Lord
   that's my question for you.

Why did you give yourself over to others?

Why did you let them make you suffer?

You could have stayed on top,
    like me,
        safe and uninvolved.

But you didn't.

So, what are you trying to tell me?
    That suffering is the only way to know real love?

Well, Lord,
    I don't suffer very well.

    And at this point in my life,
        you're the only one I trust.

I don't know how you can do it, Lord.

    But turn me loose,
        to fly out of my asbestos nest
            of shallow relationships,
        to perch on your life-giving cross
            of giving and sharing.

I think I'm ready
    to need,
    and
    to be needed.

Exploding the Categories

Where would we be without the Spirit in our lives?

    Could you imagine a relationship without Love?

    Could you imagine what it would really be like
        relating to people without ever caring?

Why is God so determined to love?

What is it about Spirit that we still need to learn?

What is it about this massive power, given to us,
    free,
    like a surprise party at the beach,
        with weather-beaten picnic tables
        bowlegged with the weight of food.

    Enough parties like that with the right people
        would make our lives different,
            colorful,
        exploding our silly grey categories
            and prejudices
        into shards of multi-colored asterisks,
            question marks
                and
            dangling
                participles.

It's an opportunity to reach out,
    reach around,
    reach within,
        and listen to that Spirit.

Then we would see what was promised:

A New Life,
   completely new,
      a new beginning,
      a life of color and excitement;
      a life that's never boring.

The choice:
   a stagnant life with black and white categories
      or
   The life of a butterfly released forever from the cocoon,
      from our tomb of everyday existence,
         to be startled by
         the colors and excitement of flight.

An Emerging God

Who is it
  who really calls me out to love
    with a wry smile
      that can only be God's mirth mark?

Is it an aura like a full moon,
  probing the canyon below with fingers of light?

Is it just a feeling, so intense with inner heat
  that you want to take off your skin
    and sit around in your bones?

Is it a longing, like an inner drum cadence,
  rumbling like a freight train through the night?

Is it just the other people around me,
  rattling in my psyche,
    like the small change of experience
    in the pockets of my memory?

  or

Is it simply something personal between us,

  between us so much
    that it almost has
      its own personality,

  between us so much
    that this personality
      seems

to
come
ALIVE
    not only
    between myself
    and
    one other person
    but
    gradually
    between myself
    and many
    other people.

PONDEROID #1

IF GOD HAS FOUND
   A PLACE TO LIVE IN HUMANITY,
      WHY CAN'T WE FIND
         OUR PLACE TO LIVE HERE TOO?

PART TWO:

EXPERIENCES, FEELINGS, REALIZATIONS, DECISIONS

Experiences

Who Is It?

Who is the mysterious presence in my life
  who is closer to me
    than I am to myself?

Who is it who's here
  when my mind is blown
    with the failure of daily life?

And what is the silence I feel
  deep in the redwood forest,
    a silence that shouts its message to me?

      In isolation,
      silence is pain

      In relationship,
      involvement is pain.
      Silence is peace.

What about the silence of my darkness?
  Can God really know my suffering?

But God is perfect.

Then who is this man, Jesus,
  rejected by authority
    misunderstood by some
      and loved by millions
        through the centuries.

This God-Man Jesus:
  he's left his mark everywhere:
    on beaches,
    in the forests,
    in people's lives,
    and on me.

Who is this friend of mine
  who touches me
    through suffering
      and ties into my suffering
        more carefully than I am even willing to?

  Who somehow takes me by the hand,
    walks me through the suffering
    and
    shows me a new life on the other side?

I guess he really is my friend,
    the person who sticks with me
    when the going goes against me.

And whenever I look for him,
  need him,
  even wonder about him,
    he is still there,
      very, very close.

A Presence Before Me

I remember a little old lady who loved to talk.

    Why is it that a person with a day to kill
        wants to spend it with someone who can't spare a minute?

I was always so busy
    that I just couldn't stick around long enough
        to hear her story.

I wonder what ever happened to that little old lady.

    Forgotten by me,
        she lost her one link to the world on the outside.
    Forgotten by me,
        she no longer touched anyone else.

I still remember her.

*   *   *

I can also remember an old man who wore braces.
    He met me out in front of church one day,
        he attired in his braces,
            and
    I attired in my Sunday-best clothes.

He asked me for a ride.

    I don't think I've ever met anyone who reflected a need
        and a message from God
            as clearly as he did that day.

I saw the contrast between my Sunday clothes
   and his braces.
I took him where he wanted to go.

*   *   *

But there have been many, many other times
   when I didn't respond,
   when I missed a need
      right in front of my face.

I realize now that there have been many times when I missed
   the chance to grow,
   when I missed the chance
      to touch God
         in the people
         around me.

Looking Back

I can remember one time when I was very young.
   I guess I was about four,
   I was playing with a little friend of mine
      out by a swimming pool half filled with water.
      Or was it half empty?

Like all kids, we went exploring the pool area,
   like hyper electric fans,
      looking this way and that.

   The shallow end was dry and inviting,
      and we were playing tag.
   Then I ran too close to the drop-off
      and I slipped into the muddy water at the deep end.

I can still remember my friend
   running off to get help,
      which arrived just in time
         in the person of a teenage neighbor
            who jumped in
            and pulled me out.

Looking back now,
   I can see God making up for damage
      I almost did to myself,
      out of the carelessness of my youth.

*   *   *

I can remember a funeral:
   my own cousin,

killed in Vietnam.
That was the saddest day of my life to that point.

I really reached out for something significant
   to give my own family.

I was searching for something to give them,
   but that day I had trouble finding it,
      because of my own grief.

But I gave my best,
   believing God put it there to give.

   It didn't come from me.

*   *   *

I can remember many happy times,

   like the day I met my first disc jockey
      at a bongo-drum-playing contest in Santa Rosa.

One of the big-time San Francisco disc jockeys was in town,
   hosting a department store promotion.

   I was so nervous,
   I sweated like a cold bottle of root beer.

But I won third place,
and had never before beat on a bongo drum in my life.

*   *   *

Were you there, Lord,
when I discovered a new rhythm in my life?

Vulnerable

One night, I went for a walk
  past the neighbor's house,
  past the corner grocery store,
    on toward the center of town:
      playground of drunks,
        disease,
        and dirty,
        dingy
        derelicts.

At first, the trouble in my own life
  had spun me
    into a web of concentration
    as I groped inward for an answer.

Paralyzed spiritually,
  I began to watch an old man tottering ahead of me
    stroking the sidewalk
      with strides of pride
      on legs of rubber.

My focus left him, briefly,
  as I considered
    the gallery of street people he passed:
    each person with his own story of pain,
      rejection,
      frustrated dreams.

Weird thing, though . . .
  as he deliriously tromped by,
    dark faces lit up,
    tense expressions relaxed.

The street people came alive to a man of weakness
 who could touch them
  in the back alleys
  of their hearts.

None of the rich
 has produced a response like that
 in the hearts
 of those in misery.

None of the world's power
 has lightened
 their load.

It took a weak,
 insecure,
 well-lathered little man
  in search of community,
   offering just enough fellowship
    to give them relief
    from the pain
    that brought them together.

There he was:
 a man . . .
 morally retarded
 and slightly regarded
  by the "good" people of the world,
 but a breath of fresh air to underachievers
  whose stale lives had created
  an underculture.

And I was *following* this guy . . .

That night, my search for an answer ended.

I found in this limp celebrity
   that weakness can touch more people
      more deeply
         than all the power-trips
            and human rip-offs
            ever devised.

That night, I discovered WHY
   God's Way to touch me was
      Poverty
      and
      a Cross.

Feelings

Feelings

Lord,
    I learned a long time ago
    not to trust my feelings.
        Feelings were bad,
           like weeds,
                those nasty uninvited plants with nine lives.
        They were always surfacing
           like a blight on my model-home lawn.

After all, everyone knew that nothing came of feelings,
    except evil.

    When I yelled as a kid,
    just because I felt like yelling,
    I was squelched:
        "Mommy has a headache."

    When I cried,
    I wasn't being very grown-up:
    I wasn't being a man.

    When I laughed,
    I upset those older people
        who had long ago forgotten how to laugh,
           forgotten how to feel.

Soon I became like them:
    no more yelling,
    no more crying,
    no more laughing.

The silence outside lied about
    the yelling,
    crying,
    laughing chaos inside.

  I had become a polite, well-groomed lie,
    living up to everyone else's hang-ups,
    but never faithful in dealing with my own.

Then some people came into my life,
  like street lights
    blasting holes in the dark.

  Maybe you sent them to me,
    or maybe they were there all the time,
    and I finally just heard them,
      like icecubes
      breaking the stillness
      in my water glass.

Anyway, they were real people,
  alive to what they saw,
    what they felt.

  They showed me life from the feeling side.

And now, Lord,
  for the first time
  like the first human,
    I see CREATION.
      I see flowers,
      I see mountains and streams.

And best of all, Lord,
  I see people,
    not just with my eyes,
    but with my feelings.

  I see PAIN
    —oh, do I see pain—
      but Lord, I see Love there too.

And now,
  for the first time,
    I think I can see
      and hear
        you.

Security

Inside of each of us
  lives the nagging fear
    that if we don't take care of ourselves,
      no one will.

This fear makes us grab selfishly
  for all the things we can get in this life.

It tells us that, for security reasons,
  we must give nothing away.

As a result, our lives are spent
  scurrying around,
    building and protecting a world
      of shallow security,

  when, all along,
    a world of security and caring
      was already built,
      already protected
      by God, Our Creator and Parent.

To refuse God's world is to deny ourselves the chance to meet a
    creative genius.

To refuse God's security is to deprive ourselves of the comfort of
    a flawless parent.

To refuse God's caring is
  to dismiss the Eternal Lover from our desperate heart,
    sentencing this ready and willing God

to wait upon our summons,
while we fret
and bluster about the evil and hurt
God allows to happen
in the only world we know.

Maybe today,
we need to quit the security chase
and to choose again
the God who loves us,
the God whose only business card
is
the lilies
of the field.

Crying Babies

Crying babies drive me crazy!

The moment comes when I least expect it,
 when my coping levels are at their lowest.

 Usually I'm trapped in a plane,
   laced to my seat,
  or
 I'm totally involved in a meal at a restaurant,
   delightfully unaware of the hurricane
    about to
    twist my innerspring
    beyond its endurance.

Then it happens:
 a 20-lb. baby
 with a 500-lb. scream;

 a noon siren,
  splitting my work-day focus in half.

My concentration vanishes,

 my peace of mind shatters;

 and my conviction that babies are cute
  and feelings are thrilling
  darts out the back door of my psyche,
   leaving behind a swirling fog of unfinished business
    and
    the nagging awareness

that what bothers me the most about crying babies
is that
I
no longer
cry.

On a Warm Sidewalk

I saw a cat the other day,
   lying there on the sidewalk,
     his fur
     furrowed
     like rumpled grey corduroy

He just kept wiggling there on his back
   totally caught up in enjoying himself
   and totally oblivious
     to the staring world passing by.

I had two feelings about that cat:

The first was the fear of looking stupid.

   Everyone knows a cool cat prances,
     slinks,
     and judges.
   He generally looks
     like he knows what he's doing.
   A cool cat *never* looks stupid.

But this cat was not cool,
   not together for a world
   of rats and mice;
     this cat was really LOOSE.

And my second feeling was jealousy.

Way down deep,
I've wanted to let it all hang out,

to roll around in life
   till flowers bloom
      from my concrete knees
   and wind whistles through my plastic elbows.

I'm tired of being lonely
   in a world
      going the opposite direction.

I want to join that cat on the warm pavement
   and leave the land where cats are "cool."

I want to free myself
   to be ONE
      with those who don't care
         what it looks like loving warm sidewalks.

Chances are,
   they won't care
      what it looks like
         loving me, either.

Pour It Out

At the end of my earthly life,

    any material possessions

    or talents

    or emotional energy

        which I haven't been willing
            to spend
            in sharing

            will accuse me

            far more devastatingly

            than the Finger of God.

Realizations

Caring

When I care about my friends,
  I try to give them time and room to grow.

When I care about myself,
  I become possessive,
    dogmatic,
    abusive,
    and self-righteous.

Caring means
  reaching out in openness,
  not holding back because of fear,

  not blaming my friend for my problems,
  not rationalizing excuses as to why I'm not growing.

When I really love others,
  I'm aware of their empty places,
    their fears,
    their needs.

I don't mock these places.

I try to fill them,
  and rejoice
    in our moments
    of coming together,
      even if it means
        standing with them
        around their emotional clothesline,
        as, together,
        we hang out our sorrows to drip dry.

My Quieter Moments

In my quieter moments
    my inner self comes forth from behind my defenses
      like dawn
        peeking from behind a tree-studded ridge.

In my quieter moments
    I sense life's rhythm,
      beating and rolling inside me, around me,
      over me,
      under me,
        and
      between me and a few special others.

In my sensitive moments
    my environment is a garden
      where I walk in the cool of early morning,
        generating magnificent thoughts,
        crafting saving plans,
          and
        feeling at one with all that is good and real.

In my gentle moments
    I am open to anyone and everyone.
      no matter what their state of ecstasy or panic.
    I am a relational person,
      alive to others,
      alert to opportunity.

It's in moments like these
    I feel myself climbing,
      my spirit soaring off

to meet
someone
crossing a timeless boundary,
descending from the beyond,
to be one with me.

It's not easy to allow myself to be quiet,
sensitive,
gentle.

Still more difficult is it
to describe these moments
to another person.
who will usually stare back
in sarcastic disbelief.

But I am approaching the time
when it's OK for others to stare,
because I am going to spend the rest of my life
climbing,
soaring,
and
meeting my friend
beyond those clouds.

Close to the Water

Water has always been
  a symbol of fascination to us,
    a mirror reflecting our lives,
      our practiced expressions,
      our occasional personality pimples,
        rising from our self-images
        like pink towers
        on our desert of fears.

Eventually,
  in approaching water,
    we come to rest
      at the center of ourselves.

We learn to relax,
  and borrow a cup of liquid calm,
    allowing our preoccupations and fears
      to descend from our focus
        like bill-collectors
        sliding
        down
        a spiral bannister.

It's here that we not only find our own center,
  musty at first,
    like an attic heavy with old memories,
  but gradually fragrant
    like the scents and sounds of stories
      waiting to be told to non-believers.

Then, like an old dog,
   listening with his nose in the dust,
      we find the presence of God.

Maybe that's why Jesus was so close to the water,
   walking around it and upon it,
   calling us out of our boat of safety
      to walk on it with him.

As we walk and talk,
   we day-trip to the center of ourselves
      and enter the mansion of the God-Within
         to share a piece of wordless friendship.

If we're going to learn the secrets of this God
   who enjoys teaching almost as much as loving,
      we need to remain
         close to the water.

Forgiveness

Thomas Edison,
    inventor of the light bulb,
        was working with his team in his lab
            to create an improved light bulb.

As the story goes,
    he handed the finished new version to a young person
        who carefully coddled it
            in his sweating hands
            up a long flight of stairs.

At the top of the stairs,
    he stumbled,
        and his trembling hands
        dropped the experimental bulb.

As the work of months shattered at his feet
    along with his confidence,
        the boy panicked.

        His eyes scurried around his face
            like alarmed ants.

        He had failed.

The whole team reassembled
    and created another prototype.

Typical of Edison's character,
    he picked up the new bulb,
    smiled,
    and handed it to the same boy.

It was a moment that changed the boy's life,
and was forever frozen
like a statue
in his memory.

And it is a classic example of the way God works.

When we fail at love
at life
at relationships,
God forgives.

When we hurt ourselves,
others,
God,
our world around us,
God forgives.

When we lose our faith in God,
we discover an even greater faith:
God's faith in us.

And at the very moment of weakness,
when our self-image,
like that light bulb,
totters on the brink of self-destruction,

God's forgiveness reminds each of us:
"You
are worth
more to me
than
what you
just did."

Decisions

Sacrifice

Thank you, TV advertising.

Now I know what my headache looks like,

    especially the headache I'm having right now.

Lord, I'd like to face it right now:
    I'm afraid of sacrifice.

    I'm afraid of anything that hurts.

When people reach out to me
    and ask me for some kind of help,
        I'm afraid!

    I'm afraid that I won't have it to give.

    Which means I'm afraid that
       you haven't given me
       anything to give.

    How could I be so stupid?

    How could I be so down on myself,
       so unwilling to recognize
          the gifts inside of me,
       so afraid to use them!

Lord, were you ever afraid of pain?

Did you ever get so afraid of pain
    that you just broke out in a sweat?

It seems to me I remember a moment in the gospel
    when you broke out in a sweat.

Well, then, maybe you would understand.

I'm afraid to commit myself to anything right now.

I really need you to give me something right now
    to help me recognize the gifts I already have,
        so I can go out and give them away to others.

Lord,
    like you who were afraid,
        I'm scared to death of what sacrifice means
        in relationships.

Marry? Each Other?

You want to marry?

Each other?

Are you crazy?

You want to go up the down escalator,
   passing all those folks
      who keep telling you from their own experience
         that marriage doesn't work
         and
         commitments like this
         cannot be kept.

There are too many uncertainties,
   temptations,
   distractions,
   hassles.

And you are telling each other
   that you will meet these obstacles together?

You are declaring before the whole world
   that what you see right now in each other
      is good enough
         for you to spend your lives together
         discovering the rest?

In your new adventure called marriage,
   you will need all the help you can get.

May God grant you
  forgiveness when you hurt one another,
  trust when you are away from one another,
  joy when you are with one another.

But, in addition,
  may you have God's best gift,
    Unconditional Love.

  When fully unwrapped and explored,
    it will make you as crazy as God.

May God's Love
  make your partnership
    a Threesome!

Turning in the Badge

Lord of my soul,
   I'm boxed in:
   the two-way door in my giving life
      has slammed in my face.

There is no way I can be everything to everyone.
   I'm stretched out too many ways.
   I'm tired and I'm making mistakes.

Lord, I'm turning in my Messiah Badge right now,
   and all my ambitions with it.

I don't want to be in charge of this world.

I haven't got the energy to hold it together.
   I must be stupid to want to be God;
   I've got too many limitations
      to be a good candidate.

I try to love people,
   and then they tell me
      I'm not doing it right.
I do the best I can,
   but it doesn't satisfy them.
      They need you, not me.

I try to understand others, but their needs boggle my mind,
   entangle my heart,
   and then we trip and fall in a heap
      on the floor.
         They need you, not me.

I try to read scripture,
   but everyone has a different interpretation.
      Does being right make everyone else wrong?

I try to understand my own feelings,
   my own direction in life
   —you know—
   do it the way everyone says it should be done.

But right now,
   I'm a very scared
   little retired Messiah.

I need something that I can't give myself.

I need you, Lord.

I need you.

Letting You Go

You're gone,
  leaving me stunned
    by the suddenness,
    the finality of your departure.

Last week,
  we were teasing each other,
    cruising down life's aisles
      like two shopping carts,
        with all the wheels going in the same direction.

Now,
  my heart hears only
    the whisk-broom sound of wind
      whipping through fallen leaves.

A part of me has been ripped away without my permission.
I am angry.

A part of me is in shock.
I am too numb to know what I really feel.

A part of me is already lonely,
  knowing I will never see your smile,
    except in my memory.

And part of me knows
  that you are alive somewhere beyond my reach.

Lord, I am in pieces.

How could you have allowed this to happen?

And yet, Lord,
   I know that my friend is with you face to face even now,
      with more happiness and love
      than I could ever hope to have given.

My friend,
   I miss you.

   I envy you.

   I will join you again someday.

   But it's so hard letting you go.

PONDEROID #2

WE
ARE
THE
PLACE
WHERE
GOD
HAPPENS

PART THREE:

LOSS,
FEAR,
HEALING,
SEASONS OF THE
HEART

Loss

How To Do the Goodbye Right

Goodbyes are the hardest part of a relationship,
  a part I can never seem to get right.

  I announce my departure to a gathering party,
    and forty-five minutes later I'm insisting—
      for the sixth time—
    that I'm going to leave;

And then, when a relationship gets too deep,
  and involvement appears on the horizon,
    my goodbyes flow too easily
      from my back-pedaling psyche.

How do I do my goodbyes?

Is there such a thing as being too close,
  and too far away?

Saying goodbyes aren't that easy,
  I mean, using them
to get the proper distance,
the right perspective
  on life,
  on people,
  on myself,
    and still not cut myself off
      from those I need,
      and who need me.

Why is it I say shallow goodbyes to those I love,
  and empty hellos to those I don't?

Lord, am I afraid of growing . . .
    out to others,
    in to myself,
    where you really live?

Lord, before I say goodbye to another scary day,
    will you open yourself to my rainy day fear,
      my darkness,
      my failure,
    and show your openness to my ugly goodbyes?

Then maybe tomorrow,
    I can do those goodbyes
      a little bit better.

The Love Lane

Lord,
   sometimes I really try to belong to the happening crowd,
     to join the fast-lane brains
       looking for high-life strife.

But, in the process, I have to open myself to their world,
   their needs,
   and what they want to do in life.

When I do,
   I feel like a newly poured pancake
     spreading out on a sizzling griddle.

Sometimes I really do feel part of their lives.

But what do I do with the times when I don't?

What do I do with the times
   when I don't even know
     what I have to give?

   Where do I put that feeling, Lord?

   Where do I put the feeling of self-worthlessness
     that creeps out of the darkness,
       and at times
       wants to strangle me?

My gifts lie within me like withered typewriters orphaned by
        computers,
   while the high performance people speed past.

But I know I'll never spend much of my life in the trendy
    express lane.

I'm just looking now for the Love Lane.

I don't like being left alone in high speed relationships,
    afraid of commitments,
    not knowing what to give.

Teach me, Lord,
    who I really am,
    and what I really have to give.

A Sick Child

How do I love the sick child in me?

    That little
        insecure,
        fearful
        aggressive child
            with a garbage-can stomach
            a road-runner mind (bleep-bleep)
            a pretzel heart
            and a telescopic ego,
                who plays in fantasy one minute,
                in reality the next.

How do I love a life that's both
    a sandy desert of howling fears
    and an ice-blue lake of mystic satisfaction
        where people are just toys to be used,
            pounded,
            discovered,
            discarded;

        then used some more
            pounded,
            protected,
            maybe even
            regarded.

How do I love the little sick child in me?

Lord, one of these days
    I'm going to get it straight;

I mean, I'll figure out
    where all those dark, lonely places are in me,
    and then
    I'll let you get in with your flashlight
    to poke around
    and see what needs fixing.

All that darkness,
    all that loneliness,
        all that selfishness:

            a screaming tracer of empty black,
            an unlit playground of razor-blade fences
                and fluorescent manholes without covers:

            the dark side
            of my emotional town
            where the sick child in me lives.

Only lately have I seen that sick child smile,
    ready again for play,
        for others,
        for life.

Lord, thank you
    for visiting softly,
    for touching firmly,
    for knowing your way around in the dark;
        you must have been there before.

Thanks so much, Lord.

I don't want to do my dark,
   sick child
   alone,
   anymore.

Losers

It's Shovers' Lane in the bargain basement.

With a dedicated fury, we are once again trapped up
            in rushing around,
    trying to achieve,
    trying to score in some way
        to make our own inner self
        feel a lot better.

Our inner eyes are lashed shut by this frenzied fantasy
    as we base our whole value system on performance and
            acquisition:

    when people do something right,
        they get ten points:
    when they blow it,
        they don't get any at all.

We lay this value system on other people,
    and begin demanding that they perform in our same style.

Then we wonder
    why we live in a society
        where there seem to be
            more losers than winners.

Here we are: a society that's rich.

We have resources that seem endless.

But has our great society produced
  more victims than successes?

And are we becoming victims of the very same frenzy
        that warns us
  to slow down.

We may be sincere,
  but we are not honest,
    not in touch with the truth about ourselves.

Maybe Being
  is a lot more important
    than Doing.

And those people who don't achieve in society,
  the "losers,"
    maybe they're not so bad off.

When they "blow it" sometimes,
  maybe they're not really
    blowing it.

Fear

Touch Me

Lord, I try so hard
   to show my best side,
   to act invincible,
   to cover up my mistakes.

If people see my worst side,
   they'd run from me
   and leave me alone,
   and I can't take that right now.

I have to wear a mask to keep my friends,
   but I hurt way down deep.

And there's no one to fix it.

Lord,
   will you help me make a few repairs
     below the waterline of my ark,
      where I keep my uglies carefully hidden?

Lord,
   touch my chicken legs,
   my vulture eyes,
   my buffalo breath,
   and my pack-rat heart.

Heal my gorilla hands,
   my beagle ears,
   my piggy nose,
   and my pelican beak.

Stretch my giraffe neck,
pump my elbows and knees dry,
and
quiet the hyena screech in my soul.

And when we're done
    walking through the barnyard
    of my fears,
        maybe I can lift my mask a little,
        and
        let others into the cured part of my life.

Lord,
    help me.

Tender in the Morning

Sometimes I don't think I'm going to get it right.
    I reach out to love,
    then I blow it,
    and I don't even know how to apologize.

Lord,
    I don't think I do my "mornings-after-the-night-befores" very
        well.

    My "nights-before" seem to get worse and worse.

    My relationships are standing by the backdoor of my memory,
        like battered boots
        whiskered with old grass cuttings.

    My "mornings-after" are getting useless.

    The point where I pick up my intimate conversations
        is worse
        than where I left off.

Lord, did you ever alienate anybody?
    I mean, say the wrong thing at the wrong time?

    Well, I have.

    And I guess I'd like to come to you today
        for a little advice:

        How do I reopen the negotiations
            after I've blown it the night before?

How do I look someone right in the eye
    after I've messed up,
        and say "Good morning!
        Let's start over."

I keep hearing your word that

    after every death
        there's a resurrection;

    after every time I blow it,
        there will be a second chance;

    even if my friend doesn't forgive,
        you will.

That makes it a lot better.

    Even with other people and their limited vision,
        even with my own limited vision,
        there's a built-in safety clause here someplace.

    If I just open myself a little more,
        try just one more time,
            you'll be there to help me through,
            to find my real
            Tenderness in the Morning.

Masks

Sometimes it comes in the morning;
  more often, late at night:

    the feeling of worthlessness;

      the nagging suspicion
      that

        at the center
        of my person
        nothing
        is
        there.

No one must know,
  so I wear a mask,
    my way of showing people
      a value I don't really feel.

But my masks look like warty frogs,
  sightless
    in my muddy puddle of relationships,

  an easy target
    for puddle-stomping kids.

The cure isn't in changing my mask,
  substituting a new one for an old one.

It's in letting someone into my emptiness,

   receiving a kiss of acceptance

      and

   being released to see
      that being empty
         only means
         being ready
            to be filled
            with
            love,
            peace,
            and
            God.

Light in the Darkness

What is it about Darkness
  that takes over my life
  and paralyzes me
    so that I can no longer move?

The Darkness from outside freezes me
  so I can't take another step forward
    for fear of tripping,
      or falling
        into a deep hole somewhere.

Even more scary is
  the Darkness inside,
    a constant season of winter skies with icicle eyes,
      keeping me from really learning to love,
      keeping me from really seeing where my life is going,
      and who is out there to love.

And that's where the Lord of Light really works in me:

Light, the power that frees me
  to move about,
the power to see
  where I'm going.

When Light,
  so mysterious in itself,
    stands before me as a Person,
  and asks me to follow,
    I will now take the risk and follow.

It doesn't take a genius
  to know that
     a Great Light
        is better than
     a Great Darkness.

Gift of Sight

Lord, I was watching all the happy people around me,
    blazing like distant campfires on the night's horizon.

But now,
    it's as if you have pulled a dark blanket over me.

Lord,
    when are you going to meet me,
        and
        stay with me long enough
            so that I can offer something back in return?

Your shadow has fallen between us,
    and lies there,
        like a tree across our path.

    Sometimes I don't even know my own needs.

    Sometimes I can't get in touch with anyone else.

Lord, I've lost contact again.

I'm blind.

    I need your touch,
        right now,

        just as those blind men did
            many years ago in the gospel stories.

Help me, Lord,
   now,

              to gain
              the
              Gift
              of
              Sight.

Healing

A Time to Heal

The family once again gathers at the dinner table
  painfully aware of the gap.

Tired and considerate parents
  peer across the table
  at the smaller children.

  The chatter flies over
    fingerpaints,
    test papers,
    and new toys.

  But the older minds wander
  and the younger minds wonder.

No one says the obvious:

The teenagers are out again,
  out
  searching for community in a lonely world,
    for direction in an aimless peer group,
    for acceptance in a competitive culture.

Somewhere,
  along the jumbled journey for independence,
  there was a confused shouting match
    with equally confused parents.

And then, because
  no one knew what to say
  or, even, how to speak,
  the important words were never said.

Tonight,
   suffering the empty chairs around the family table,
      the feelings are still there,
      but this time, so are the words:

      "Come home; we miss you."

Lonely-Looking Sky

The owl is finished for the night.

The deer begin flowing down the hillside with the morning fog.

In the city, the necklace of street lights
    wraps itself around the darkened monument to fallen heroes,
    while soggy solitaries
    stagger by
    in a lonely search for happiness.

There is no more lonely place than
    pre-dawn darkness
    looking for
    the first light from the rising sun.

Across the lonely-looking sky,
    the night's emptiness stretches forth its arms
    to drink the pink-liquid light,
        reassuring itself that
        the dark terror of nocturnal fears
            will fade before daylight's awesome power.

Who is it
    who could set before us
    such a clear message
    about our lives?

Only the One
    who created the consoling mystery of light over darkness,
        of gentleness over harshness,
            and
        of vision over blindness from within.

The sky is lonely
　　only
　　　　for the sun
　　　　　　to run onstage
　　　　　　to complete its existence
　　　　　　　　and
　　　　　　give us the next presentation.

Pushing Away

Sleep is the door
    to my basement of spiritual terrors,

    a door I can close as the summary of my day's encounters
      swirls toward me like a herd of munching tornadoes
      ripping up my feeling structure
        and
      flinging it into some God-forsaken, foggy swamp.

As my sleep-door closes
    on my ever increasing realization
      of my role in people's lives,

    I find myself—at last—pushing away from the day,
      back into my interior world
      where the skies are always blue,
      where the beaches are always warm,
        and
      where the good guys all wear white hats.

This is my "other side"
    where fantasy becomes reality
      and reality becomes symbolic:

      "DREAMLAND,"
      fully equipped with the latest in Fairy Godmothers

I'm only now hearing my need to be alone
    as an option truly acceptable in my life.

Compulsive fantasy is an illness to be feared.

But I no longer fear the world of chosen fantasy
   where trips to the inner world, naturally induced,
   can bring me to an encounter with myself
      and with God
   that cannot be explained adequately to anyone.

     For someone who hasn't been there,
       there are no words of explanation.
     For someone who has been there,
       there is no need for such words.

Pushing away
   is now becoming part of my daily routine.

It's my pause in the day to collect myself.

It's my chance to ponder the wisdom of the Scriptures.
     and
   to drink the energy
     that seeps out of patient redwoods.

   This same power glides toward me from people
     who seems to know and understand
       that my destiny is still
       between
       me
       and
       God.

It's a course continuously being charted
   during our encounters
     within my whited sepulchre:

still black in places,
still holding some dead bones,
   but
still—as always—a great place
   to push away from death
   and
   to greet the world
   with my resurrected
   NEW LIFE.

Command the Sun

Ever have one of those days
  when nothing goes right,
  when everything you try fails,
  when your best friend rejects you,
  when your soul screeches through your being
    like a broken muffler dragging on asphalt?

Pick up the daily newspaper.
Find the weather page.
Locate the next day predicted to have clear weather.
Identify to the exact minute the time of that day's sunrise.

Be sure to rise early on that specific morning
    while it is still dark.

  Go to a beach,
    a lake,
    a river,
      or
    any scenic spot of your choice.

  Watch in the dark velvet silence,
    as the morning sky brightens from blue,
      to pink,
      to orange.

Then,
  thirty seconds before the scheduled time of the sunrise,
    raise up your arms
      with hands pointing
      toward the scarlet horizon,

and
Command the Sun To Rise.

And the sun will obey you.

If necessary,
or just for the thrill of it,
repeat this sequence for the sunset.

Command the Sun To Set.

And on another day,
when the weather is horrible,
when your heart is heavy,
when your soul is dark with fear,
when you even find yourself homesick
for someplace you've never been,

stand up in your darkened space,
raise up your arms once again,
with your hands
pointing away from you,
and

Command God To Love You.

And even God will obey you.

*Seasons of
the Heart*

Shalom

The trees are jostled by the wind,
   prompting them
   to fling another flurry of farewell kisses of red and gold.

Out on a limb,
   the cocoon is quiet,
      the bug
      wrapped
      in a homespun security blanket.

      Uninvolved?

      Hardly.

      Only waiting
         changing,
         becoming.

Someday, a seasonal signal,

   then a blooming moment,

      a resurrection flag-waving
         as wings unfurled
         proclaim new life,
            new vision,
            new mobility.

   Only a crazy caterpillar
      hearing a tone
      no other insect hears

dares
defy the world of strugglers
    and
peacefully
wrap
    and
wait

"losing" an old identity
    to possess the new.

Thanksgiving

Lord,

   I just want to say "thanks" for being patient with me.

A lot of my friends get so uptight with me
   when I run
   in and out of relationships
   trying to find myself.

In my lonely search,
   I find I fall out of relationships
     more easily than I get in.

   But that's me right now, I guess.

Some people can't accept that in me yet.

You're different, Lord, from all the people around me.

You don't force the issue.

   You have the patience of forever.

   You have carved out mountains with glaciers of ice.

   You have seen the giant redwood grow from a seed.

   You, Lord, have been the friend I have always needed,
     offering a relationship, ,
     but never forcing it.

All along, you have been the one there,
 ready when I was,
 offering what I could take,
 taking what I could offer,
 and turning it back into
  more of a gift to me
   than to you.

Thanks for being with me
 until I was grown up enough
  to be with you.

I think I know now what it means
 to be inter-dependent.

You're all right!

Christmas Star

Across the world once again,
   a star is in our sky,
   a gift is in our hearts:
   it's Christmas.

Right here at home
   our highway is our backbone,
   our rivers, our arms and legs.
   The forest is our clothing.
   The ocean is our blood.

As a people, we have known
   struggle,
   isolation,
   darkness,
     and
   bitterness.

But more importantly,
   we have also found
     success,
     security,
     happiness,
       and
     one another.

It's Christmas once again:
   time to focus on
     what makes light overcome darkness
       and
     love overcome emptiness.

It's time to believe once more that
   no matter how battered our lives are,
   no matter how well off we are materially,
      there is still someone
         who knows our darkness and lights it,
         who knows our hurt and heals it.

It's a moment for healing,
   and we really need it this time.

Healing is the medicine that can close the wounds
   between parent and child,
      brother and sister,
      government and people.

Healing comes from God
   directly or indirectly.

We must do what we can do;

God does the rest.

Merry Christmas.

New Year's Resolution

Out of icy clouds and frosty peaks,
   a river winds down the mountain,
      pouring into gorges,
      and spreading fingers of latticework
         through soggy green fields.

The river knows where it's going;
   it has its own momentum.

Overhead, a bird loiters on quiet currents of air,
   clean, fresh air,
      then cruises easily across scenic vistas.

The New Year is ours once again.

But for mountains and birds,
   streams and fish,
      nothing is really new.

We are the ones who need a New Year
   to leave behind old mistakes,
   to heal broken relationships,
   to find more sources of energy to convey us to new places,
      new relationships,
      new beginnings.

We begin this year jealous of majestic birds
   who know their energy source
   and use it wisely.

We begin this year angry at others
    who have wasted our energy,
      but conscious, when we are honest with ourselves,
        that we have wasted our own material energy
          and what's worse,
            our psychic, spiritual energy as well.

Waiting for the Petroleum Cartels,
    or the Oil Companies
      won't help us solve
        the real energy crisis:
          the Love Crisis in our lives.

Loneliness is an energy crisis.

Emptiness is an energy crisis.

Hate is an energy crisis.

  Our hearts are the only fuel pumps:
    they never run dry,
    they just get tired.

On this great Morning After the Year Before,
  it is good to know that
    Life is always new,
    Love is always ready
      to boost,
      to cheer,
      to forgive,
        and
      to begin again.

ZAPOID #1

There's not much difference between
a person who can't see
and
a person who won't see.

PART FOUR:

SEARCH,
DOWNER
CELEBRATIONS,
DISCOVERY,
UPPER CELEBRATIONS

Search

Stop and Wait

There are so many street people today
  cruising slowly like snails
    towing their belongings on their backs.

Where am I going?

What am I clinging to?

What do I really hope
  will fill the emptiness
    down deep inside myself?

If I could have anything I wanted in this life,
  free,
    what would I take?

How far would I really have to travel to get it?

It just seems that I am so often trying to flee
  instead of heading into
    relationships.

I'm running away from people,
  running away from God,
  running away from the very Love
    who could
    fill
    my emptiness.

Maybe the best way to search is
  to stop and wait

for God's mysterious presence
   to invade my darkness,
   to come in,
   to search around,
      and
   to choose the best time and place
   to open the conversation.

God somehow knows
   where my darkness is
      even better than I do.

Reach for the Sky

Where do people get it?

Where does love come from?

Why does love totally preoccupy my needs,
    and so overwhelm everything else I do
    that nothing has any meaning without it?

Who is this masked marauder in my life
    who steals into my presence in the dark
    and shows up in the light
    as a two-armed holdup:

the Great Heart Robbery:

"Reach for the Sky!"

Lord, sometimes I think you play games with me—
    you know,
    fool with my mind,
    tinker with my life.

But that's OK.

Since I've come to you for help,
    my life is moving again.

I'm getting better mileage
    and less pollution.

I'm having fun again.

And I suspect that it's my games you're playing
    entering my life where I need you,
    teaching me some of your games
      like
      the Great Heart Robbery.

But where do you come from?

Where is your hideout?

Where do you go when I can't sense you?

I really want to know.

Something To Say

Have you ever been caught
  in a conversation
  with nothing to say?

Staring at the other person?

Trying to say just about anything?

Any words that could come out
  would be better
    than the silence in your own heart.

Have you ever tried to listen to someone
  who had nothing to say?
    Boring.

I've been thinking about my prayer life lately.

It just seems that when God appears in my life,
  I don't know what to say.

I don't know how to start the conversation.

I don't know how to respond
  to what I hear and see.

So often, my own prayer life is usually
  a feeble attempt
  to manipulate God:

"Dear Lord, would you mind rearranging the universe
  to suit my plan?

Would you mind using some of your almighty power
  while I direct you with my almighty brain?"

God must laugh at that!

Sometimes in prayer,
  I just have nothing to say.

  And when an awkward silence
    is the only thing
    I can offer God,
    maybe that's fine.

Actually,
  when I think about it,
    God is the only one
      who really has anything significant to say.

      I could just sit
        and
        listen.

The Crossing

Through the gold-soaked mists of early morning,
    the city bus trundles down the street
    like a tired monster,
    inhaling and exhaling its passengers.

It's the morning commute,
    oddly named "rush hour,"
        when traffic hardly moves,
            breaking out constantly
                in a rash of red taillights.

    The driver,
        with all the charisma of a boiled turnip,
        brings the bus to its last stop,
            the Ferry Terminal,
    and with a sigh of airbrakes,
        the bus belches the remaining passengers onto the ramp.

Flashing wallets,
    tickets,
    tokens
    and money,
    the crowd moves through the turnstile
        and onto the boat,
            parting like the teeth of a giant opening zipper,
                some to the upper deck,
                the rest to the enclosed lower deck.

The crew releases the restraining ropes
    at the command of the First Mate,
        whose voice could steer ships
            through a dense fog.

On this journey,
    some passengers have positioned themselves upstairs
        to be out on deck,
        dressed for the morning chill,
        stimulated by an inner drive
            to see the sights of the city,
                the other boats,
                the birds,
                the other passengers.

    They are enjoying the ride.

Downstairs,
    other people are slumped in their seats,
        heads bowed like buffalo fording a river,
        dragging their reflections with them,
        transfixed by the steam from their cups of coffee,
        contemplating the tasks awaiting them across the water.

This ferry,
    just another passenger vehicle,
    is an archetype of our society.

The world is filled with people on two levels.

    There are those who are enjoying
        as much of the journey as possible,

    and there are those who just want
        to get across.

Downner
Celebrations

Sidetrack

For years,
   I sat on the sidetrack of life,
      watching other people's trains go by,

      watching the expresses going fast,
         the trains with heavy loads going by slowly.

   But I wasn't moving at all.

   I had gotten out of their way,
   and there I was,
      a vehicle carrying nothing
         and going nowhere.

No amount of wishing on my part
   would push me out onto the main line.

I needed someone to come along
      and pull me back into life.
      And someone did.

It took a lot of passenger trains and freight trains going by
   before someone noticed
      and stopped
      and backed onto my siding
      and then latched on.

I stayed close to that person for quite a while,
   and I borrowed a lot of my formulas about life
   from my rescuer.

But then I was dropped off onto another siding.

Only, I was discovered again
   and towed along some more.

After living on many sidetracks now,
   I've come to appreciate other people sitting there,
     feeling very empty
     and very unsure about
       who might come along
       to help them continue the journey.

These days,
   when I'm passing by,
     I always look to the sidetracks,
     always at the people who are standing there
       needing somebody to reach out a hand
       needing somebody to give them a lift
         to the next place they're going.

Now,
   I've been really at home on the main line,
     but I'm still picking up people
       from the sidetracks.

White Hats—Black Hats

It seems like a garbage truck
   visits my mind
   five times a day,
     dumping on me facts and relationships
      I just can't handle.

There I sit in the middle of my pile of debris:

Future Shock on a Scrap Heap.

My fried conscience activates its screaming "faults alarm,"
   a growing ritual
   that's far too habitual.

As it all hits me,
   I sort and sift
     and
   I categorize what I see around me.

   I throw good stuff into white boxes,
     bad stuff into black boxes.

   Since I am in the center of my viewpoint,
     everything that crosses into my view
     is judged
      by my standards of acceptance,
     and then delivered
      to the right category.

Lord, in your kingdom,
   are there really white boxes and black boxes?

Are there really sheep and goats,
   good guys and bad guys,
   white hats and black hats?

I know,
by my standards,
there are many winners and losers in life.

But I'm tired of narrow judgments.

Please, Lord,
   I know there is right and wrong.

But no more divisive categories;
   just people to love.

Troubled One's Day

Today is the Troubled One's Day.

Today is the Day of the Weary One,
  the Beleaguered One,
  the Wronged One,
  the Unfulfilled One.

Today is the Day for those
    whose dreams have not yet come true,
    whose plans have not worked,
    whose hands have not created:

  the Day for those
    whose faith has been muted,
    whose hopes have been dashed,
    whose love has been rejected.

Today is our day, my day:

  ours because there is a part of all of us
    that cries out for more growth,
      more happiness
        than what has come so far;

  mine because the suffering is so intense,
    so lonely
      that no one else could possibly want to share it.

And Today, into my life walks another One
  who, like me, is Troubled,
    Weary,

Wronged,
Unfulfilled;
who has dreamed more anxiously than I,
planned more carefully,
worked more diligently;

whose faith has been challenged
whose hopes have been ridiculed,
whose love has been misunderstood.

And this person says to all the "me's" in the world:
"Come with me:
we are going to put this Troubled One
to death.
We are going to kill the part of me that cannot grow
so that all of me can be free to have Life,
and have it more abundantly."

And so Today I offer my sacrifice:
and my sacrifice, my gift, is my Fear:
not a very pretty offering,
but it's a part of me;

And I can now say to my Friend:
"Change it;
Make it more than it is now."

And Today, the Day of the Troubled One,
a Change,
a Consecration takes place
that can renew the whole world.

Today,
    the Troubled One dies
        and my Fear turns to Peace,

        my Peace brings Joy,

        and my Joy becomes my Life.

The Mind of Jesus Dies

The light goes out of a child's eyes
  snuffed out by poverty,
    disease,
    ignorance,
    indifference,
    abuse,
     and
    the daily lack of love:

  The Face of Jesus dies.

An unsafe coal mine explodes,
  trapping thirty miners inside
    in a morbid death ceremony,
  leaving thirty families
    with no one to care for them:

  and the Arms of Jesus die.

An old woman, crippled with arthritis,
  no longer able to come to be used
    as a baby-sitter for the grandchildren,
  no longer able to walk anywhere,
  sits in a rest home—alone—in a wheelchair,
    forgotten by the family who "needed" her a year ago:

  and the Legs of Jesus die.

An alcoholic lies wasted on Second Street,
  his liver gone,
  his hopes crushed,

his stomach empty,

longing for everything,
filled with nothing:

and the Belly of Jesus dies.

The student faced with an uncertain future,
uncertain relationships,
an uncertain culture that scorns belief,

pelted in class with the decivilization
and destruction of life as we know it,
wanders into a drugged escape:

and the Mind of Jesus dies.

People pass one another on the street with a vacant stare.

Christians refuse an extended hand in their own churches.

Whole generations throwing emotional rocks at one another,
each calling the other "useless."

The beat no longer goes on;

the Heart of Jesus has stopped;

the Body of Jesus dies;

and Resurrection is our only hope.

Someone once said, "The Spirit gives life."

And the Spirit of Jesus,
   untouched by death,
   roams the world
      the way a smile roams a face,
      the way the sun tans the working arm,
      the way blood circulates in the walking leg,
      the way food nourishes the hungry stomach,
      the way Truth refreshes the mind,
      the way Love stimulates the beat of the heart.

But the Spirit needs a body to live in,
   a body to give life to.

And we have a Body that needs life,
   needs it more than ever.

I wonder if we can get Body and Spirit together soon,
   and produce another
   Easter Resurrection.

WHEN YOU'RE READY

God is not
    "You should . . ."
      or
    "We must . . ."
      or
    "They'd better . . ."
      or
    "I ought . . ."

God is
    "I AM"
    here;
    now
    or
    later:
    when you're ready.

Discovery

Where Does God Live?

Think of all the money
   that has gone into
      the buildings of Christian worship,

      buildings that have been the source of inspiration
         throughout the centuries.

And think of the temple
   to human misery and poverty
      which has outlasted the strongest buildings.

And then you will know
   why God
   took up a permanent dwelling
   in the human temple.

In Jesus Christ,
   God resides in a poor person,
      becoming the economic problem we have never solved.

   God resides in a rich person,
      becoming the resource problem we have never solved.

   God resides in an abandoned person,
      becoming the emotional problem we have never solved.

   God resides amazingly in me,
      becoming the self-image problem I have never solved.

Where does our God live?

Find a problem.

God will already be there.

Nerve Endings

Someone else beheld an almond tree, and discovered God.

But I know of no almond trees.

So I said to the apple tree: "Speak to me of God,"
   and the apple tree blossomed!

I spoke to the sky and said, "Speak to me of God,"
   and it rained.

I spoke to the road,
   and it accepted my wheels.

I spoke to the puppy,
   and he wagged his tail.

   Then I spoke to the grass,
      and it offered me a place to rest.

   I spoke to the telephone pole,
      and it held up its wires of communication.

   I spoke to the bird,
      and it soared a little higher.

      I spoke to the path,
         and it showed me a way.

      I spoke to the child,
         and he offered to play with me.

I spoke to the sun,
    and it continued to shine.

I spoke to the water,
    and it refreshed me.

It seemed that everything I spoke to
  spoke about God
    because it spoke from its own identity.

From all ages, the world has been speaking from its core,
  while many of us,
  our ears jaded to sound,
  our eyes blurred by achievement,
    ponder God as an abstract thought,
    and then complain about God's lack of presence.

Finally, on my journey,
  I spoke to my heart and said:
    "Speak to me of God,"
      and my heart cried out for Love.

Discovery

Summer is the settling of the Winter of Discontent.

And digging my way from my cave of spiritual hibernation,
    I find that the summer sun has shed light
        on a few questions I used to wonder about.

It just came to me one day that

    To Believe is to reach out in the darkness
        and ask for a cure.

    To Hope is to be in the constant state of discovery.

    To Love is to be responsive to someone,
        to sacrifice oneself for someone,
        to risk and to share.

    To Pray is to receive God's communications,
        to be attentive,
        to listen,
        to respond.

    To Be in God's Grace is to let things and people happen to us
        while God slips in among them.

    To worship is to celebrate all of this as best we can.

    For we are reminded once again:
        "Nothing is profane
        for those
        who know how to see."*
* Teilhard de Chardin

Caterpillar

So many things in life are a paradox.

Behold the little caterpillar
  crawling along the ground,

    a little, nameless somebody
      who always seems
        to be stepped on,
        run over,
        or eaten.

But this complex creature carries a script within
    that speaks
    of greater things
    than a rumbling, bumbling caterpillar.

It's the power to become a butterfly,
    a potential
    that can be fulfilled
    only through apparent death.

In this fuzzy bug,
    we are shown once again
    that the Spirit of God
    always communicates.

We are called to follow our own inner script,
    a role that keeps us
      hanging onto our promised life,

even when we look as if we are dead in a cocoon;
waiting until the moment we are released
　in color
　　and
　　in flight.

Upper
Celebrations

Joy Song

There's got to be more to life
   than what we've experienced so far:
      fifty billion maggots can't be all wrong!

What if they gave a hell, and nobody came?

What happened to the "hundredfold" in this life?

Don't tell me the Greatest Story Ever Told
   has a crummy ending!

There has to be Joy somewhere in the middle of all this mess—
   a Joy that's aware of pain;
   a Joy that recognizes grief, but moves beyond it;
   a Joy that says it's OK to cut loose and be me,
      and like it!

I've seen flashes of Joy
      in rebellious flowers blooming in the rain;
      in newborn babies hosting their own inaugural bawl;

      in delirious cats swimming in a fishpond;
      in children making mud pies;

      in men kissing their wives;
      in square-dancing teenagers;

      in grandparents holding a spoiling bee;
      in sunsets that don't know when to quit;

flashes that say:
  somewhere,
  someone's really enjoying this life
    and having more fun than just a joke
      and more peace than just laughter,
      more experience than just the passing
      of a good time.

Joy is myself
  in touch with the best of everything,

  even when it only happens
    once in a while.

The Guitar Player

Listen to any music,
    and you will hear something stir in your soul.

But listen to the Guitar Player,
    and you will hear your soul played out of control.

    Your spirit will know simplicity in the midst of complexity.

    This riff will streak like sunlight across a cloudy sky,
        like a voice that doesn't have to talk to be heard:
        like a hand that doesn't have to touch to be felt.

There's something strangely familiar in that melody,
    like hearing a person you've seen for the first time,
    and yet you know you've met him somewhere before:
        The Guitar Player.

This Guitar freaks its way across time-honored arrangements,
    lifting us from beds of apathy,

        percolating our private puddles with a summer downpour,

        resurrecting us from premature death.

The flying, flexing fingers

    construct a strange harmony
        between the old and the new;
        between left and right,
            black and white,

joining the empty to the full,
and the crawling to the running,

bringing self-awareness to the selfish,
relationship to the lonely,
life to the dead.

There's something strange about the Guitar Player
in this song

something strange,
like the voice of God.

Listen to any Music, but be ready.

The Guitar Player
will play your soul
again.

The Curtain Goes Up

Light's early morning fingers
   chase shadows across the treetops
   as sunshine once again takes possession of the day.

Gracefully, the grey night surrenders her starry cloak
   to the Pillar of Fire journeying from the East.

Joyous birds streak across pastel skies,
   chirping the musical accompaniment
      to the full, sensual drama
      that all creation is once again presenting.

Forest animals move shyly to their places
   as rocks glisten and giant redwoods tremble.

It is the people who perhaps have missed a cue,
   playing observers
   when actually we are fully ourselves
      only as participants speaking the crucial love-lines
         which highlight the central theme
         within this magnificent scenario.

The theme is caring for ourselves,
   for others,
   for all of life.

The plot handed to us is a mystery of love received
   and then passed on to others.

We speak what we hear spoken to us.

We give what is given to us.

We seek out in others what was called forth from us.

As the day breaks once again,
   warmth creeps back into our psyches,
   reminding us that we can still be as fully alive
     and fully loved
     as we allow ourselves to be.

Heartbeat

The sound of the human heartbeat
   is one of the most thrilling sounds in existence.

It is the core of a person's rhythm
   in stride with the pulse of life.

The sound of one person's beat is in foot-tapping
      or
   finger-snapping.

Another person keeps time with word-cadence
      or
   head-bobbing.

Some swing,
   some bounce,
      some wiggle.

Our neighborhood rises to another morning
   checking its pulse.

   The day will be upbeat,
      downbeat,
         or
   offbeat.
   But everyone will move to the beat of an inner drum.

From all ages,
   mystics have spent their lives measuring their heartbeats,
   their pulses,
   their rhythm.

The inner journey toward God
   will always lead us pilgrims
   across the plaza of our own emotional town
   in search of our spiritual identity.

The day we discover our own inner pulse
    beating in harmony with another,
we can paint the world
   the color of the heart.

  For then we will then know
    from personal experience
      that
      Love
      only has
      a first name.

A REAL BLESSING

May your shit turn to fertilizer.
May the wait be worth the smell.
May your journey end in heaven.
While you send your fears to hell.

Don Kimball is the founder and President of Cornerstone Media, Inc., Santa Rosa, California. He has been the Coordinator of Youth Ministry for the Diocese of Santa Rosa. With 25 years of experience in radio, Don Kimball is the disc jockey of *Reflection: Music with a Message*, a popular rock music radio show dealing with relationships.

Don Kimball is the author of the multi-media series *Driftwood: Prayers for Beached Travelers*, and another recent book *A Spirituality of Relationships* (Don Bosco). He is co-author of the *Genesis II* High School Program and has written two books for teenagers and for parents of teenagers: *Who's Gonna Love Me?* (for teenagers) and *How Will You Know I Love You?* (for parents of teens) (Tabor Publishing).

As an adjunct professor, Don has taught at the University of San Francisco (California), Notre Dame University (Indiana), St. John's University (New York), University of Dayton (Ohio), La Salle University (Pennsylvania), and Seattle University (Washington). He is a popular speaker at religious education institutes and youth rallies across the U.S. and Canada.

DRIFTWOOD Audio and Video productions are available for your viewing and listening pleasure.

DRIFTWOOD: SCENIC VIDEO PRAYERS FOR BEACHED TRAVELERS
SERIES ONE: EXPECTATIONS FRUSTRATIONS MOOD TIDES QUESTIONS

The *Driftwood* videos offer reflections and music set against spectacular full-color photography of sea and land. The four videos in Series One each address a different area of human restlessness, a time when we feel adrift from God. The reflections are accompanied by soft, soothing instrumental music and are set against timeless and haunting videography. These images, mainly of sea and shore, emphasize that each of us is a piece of driftwood being smoothed by life's rough waves. More than just a taping of Part One of the *Driftwood* book, these high-quality videos combine sight and sound for a total meditative experience—perfect to encourage a quiet mood, initiate a discussion, or explore one's spirituality.

4-20 minute video cassettes.
Accompanying video guide booklet.   8184-3 $89.95

DRIFTWOOD: AUDIO PRAYERS FOR BEACHED TRAVELERS
SERIES ONE: EXPECTATIONS FRUSTRATIONS MOOD TIDES QUESTIONS

The soundtrack to the videos, containing both the spoken reflections and original theme music, comes in two handy audio tapes—a total of 80 minutes of high-quality listening. The tapes can be used in the above settings, as well as over a P.A. system or in a personal Walkman. An audio guide booklet includes the words to the reflections.

2-40 minute audio cassettes.
Accompanying audio guide booklet.   8183-5 $29.95

ORDER COUPON   Order from your local bookstore or PAULIST PRESS
997 Macarthur Blvd., Mahwah, NJ 07430 (201)825-7300

Send _____ copy of DRIFTWOOD Video, Series One
4-20 minute cassettes with video guide booklet 8184-3 $89.95
Send _____ copy of DRIFTWOOD Audio, Series One
2-40 minute cassettes with audio guide booklet 8183-5 $29.95
For shipping add $4.50 for the Video; $2.50 for the Audio.
(California buyers please add applicable sales tax)

Total _____

Name _____

Street _____

City/State/Zip _____